All rights reserved by Lemniscaat LCC • New York
and Lemniscaat b.v. • Rotterdam, 2013
© illustrations: Charlotte Dematons, 2012
Library of Congress Cataloging-in-Publication Data is available.
ISBN 13: 978-1-935954-28-6
Printing and binding: Proost n.v., Turnhout, Belgium

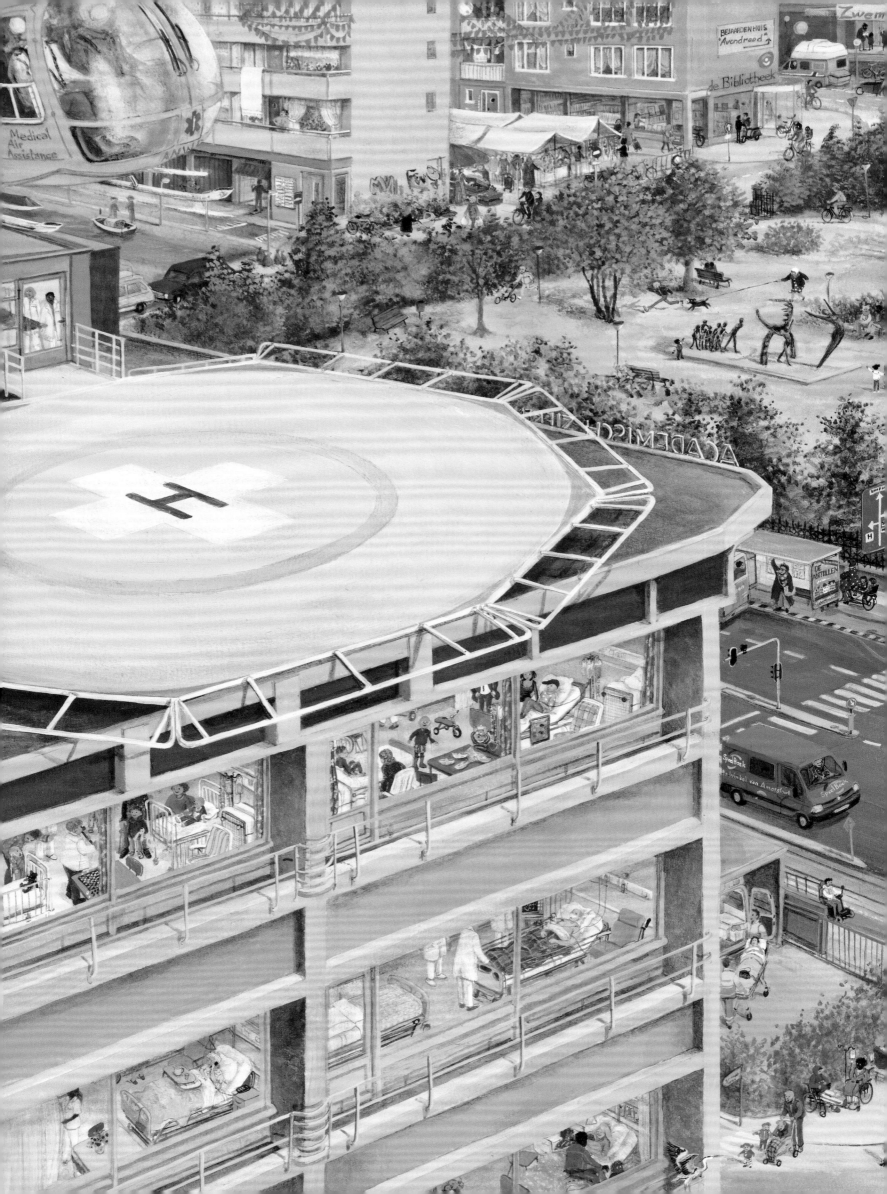

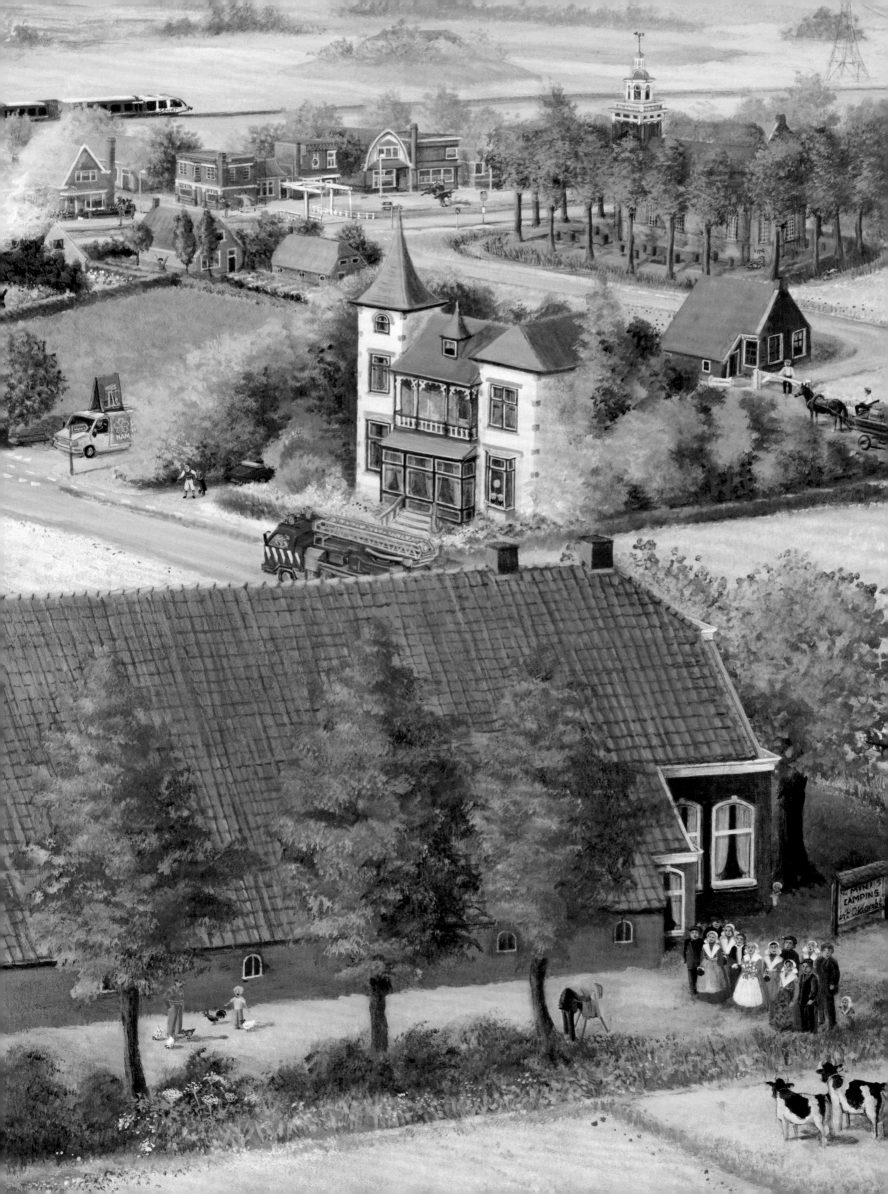